FLUID PENTATONICS

BY TIM QUINN

MBGU · MEL BAY GUITAR UNIVERSITY ·

BOOK 2

84 MELODIC STUDIES FOR ROCK GUITAR

ONLINE AUDIO

1	Study 1	24	Study 2	47	Sequence 10	70	Study 2
2	Study 2	25	Study 3	48	Sequence 11	71	Study 3
3	Study 3	26	Study 4	49	Sequence 12	72	Study 4
4	Study 4	27	Study 5	50	Sequence 13	73	Study 5
5	Study 5	28	Study 1	51	Sequence 14	74	Study 1
6	Accompaniment	29	Study 2	52	Sequence 15	75	Study 2
7	Accompaniment	30	Study 3	53	Fingering 1	76	Study 3
8	Study 1	31	Study 4	54	Fingering 2	77	Study 4
9	Study 2	32	Study 5	55	Fingering 3	78	Study 5
10	Study 3	33	Study 1	56	Fingering 4	79	A Mixolydian
11	Study 4	34	Study 2	57	Fingering 5	80	D Mixolydian
12	Study 5	35	Study 3	58	Study 1	81	Study 1
13	Study 1	36	Study 4	59	Study 2	82	Study 2
14	Study 2	37	Study 5	60	Study 3	83	Study 3
15	Study 3	38	Sequence 1	61	Study 4	84	Study 4
16	Study 4	39	Sequence 2	62	Study 5	85	Study 5
17	Study 5	40	Sequence 3	63	Study 1	86	Study 6
18	Study 1	41	Sequence 4	64	Study 2	87	Study 7
19	Study 2	42	Sequence 5	65	Study 3	88	Etude 1
20	Study 3	43	Sequence 6	66	Study 4	89	Etude 2
21	Study 4	44	Sequence 7	67	Study 5		
22	Study 5	45	Sequence 8	68	Accompaniment		
23	Study 1	46	Sequence 9	69	Study 1		

To Access the Online Audio Go To:
www.melbay.com/20681BCDEB

Visit us on the Web at www.melbay.com — E-mail us at email@melbay.com

acknowledgements

A heartfelt thanks goes out to all the teachers who profoundly impacted my own playing and learning…thank you Jack Petersen, Dan Haerle, Rich Matteson, and Tom Johnson at the University of North Texas, as well as to my teachers at Berklee College of Music. To the musicians who have been so inspiring…Steve Morse, Pat Martino, John Coltrane, Eric Johnson, Chick Corea, Jimi Hendrix, Frank Zappa, Barney Kessell, Wes Montgomery, Stevie Ray Vaughan, Albert King, Jeff Beck, Steve Vai, Dexter Gordon, Cannonball Adderly, Joe Satriani, Igor Stravinsky, Eddie Van Halen, Al DiMeola, Greg Howe, Joe Pass, Robben Ford, Vinnie Moore, Allan Holdsworth, and Carlos Santana; for the teachings of Paramahansa Yogananda; also to Bill Bay and the fine staff at Mel Bay Publications, Inc.; to Bruce Saunders for his caring engraving; to Dave Austin and George Sanchez for their generous assistance; to Josquin DePres at Track Star Studios for much inspiration and guidance; to the many students who have been indispensable in helping me streamline these materials; to my parents who provided the music education and encouraged the young performer; and especially to my wife, Mari, who lovingly tolerated the thousands of hours with me at the guitar while I formulated these concepts…thank you.

contents

Each example in this book is numbered, referring to the CD Track number.

introduction

FLUID PENTATONICS is a scientific manual for developing fast and fluid pentatonic motion on the guitar that connects and constantly shifts between the traditional five pentatonic "box" scale fingerings, using position-shifting slides, hammer-ons, and pull-offs. Traditional pentatonic scales on the guitar consist of five "box-like" scale fingerings, each fingering having two notes on every string, which creates their box-like nature. These traditional patterns are extremely important and useful, but they can be very restrictive. This book is all about overcoming the restrictive nature of pentatonic boxes by developing fast and flowing whole neck fluidity and freedom that continually shifts between and connects the traditional five pentatonic box scale fingerings.

FLUID PENTATONICS develops fast pentatonic motion that defies stylistic categorization, which can be applied to all styles of music without sounding "bluesy". Blues-style pentatonic soloing is extremely useful, but it can also sound rather dated if that's all you do with pentatonic scales. This book unlocks an almost magical way of moving through pentatonic scales that is fast and flowing, which could perhaps be better described as "modern-age" pentatonic motion, because it is definitely NOT bluesy in its sound.

In addition, *FLUID PENTATONICS* also has two chapters that develop interesting alternative takes on the pentatonic scale. These studies, in the sections on "Hexatonic" and "Dominant Pentatonic" soloing, offer two vital extensions/variations on the traditional pentatonic scale. These chapters present two collections of extremely powerful and practical melodic studies that are indispensable for developing a modern pentatonic sound.

By playing the patterns and studies herein on a regular basis, for weeks, months, and years, the player's control over the instrument will continue to unfold and grow ever more ferocious and powerful. This book is the second book in the **'FLUID SOLOING SERIES'**, a unified set of four books that develops different aspects of whole neck fluid motion on the guitar. The two "Comprehensive" soloing etudes at the very end of this book are included to demonstrate some of the techniques from the other three books, as well as the techniques in this one, all used in combination to create an exciting soloing style that is flowing and varied in its melodic patterns. If you like the content of this book, check out the other books in the series as well. Happy pentatonics, friends, and may the force be with you!

a few important points about this book

1. Most of the examples in this book are repetitive exercises. After you've learned them as written, try starting the melodic patterns from a different location. For example, if a pattern begins with an ascending motion, and then goes into a descending motion (so that it can start over), try starting the pattern at the point at which it begins to descend instead. This greatly increases the usefulness of the pattern.

2. When working on a given pattern, memorize it so you can direct all of your visual and mental attention toward your hands and the guitar. Reading the exercise off the paper requires one third of your attention. Better to play a pattern from memory with eyes on the hands, thereby putting your mental energy into the execution of the passage, rather than into reading it.

3. When fingering two consecutive notes that lie on adjacent strings in the same fret, use the same finger for both notes. Do not lift the fingertip off of the first note as you go to the next note, but rather, roll the tip of the finger onto the second note, so that the finger never actually lifts off of the fretboard.

4. Be sure to read the appendix at the end of the book, entitled **GUIDELINES FOR USING THIS BOOK.** Here you will find much useful insight, including a detailed description of strict alternate picking and its application.

5. Cultivate the ability to play musical passages as a result of *imagining the sound.* Sing the melodies internally as you **let your hands play the notes**. Let go of intellectual control. Get used to playing music purely as a result of channeling the sound you hear in your head, as opposed to it being an exercise in physical execution. After all, this IS music. The best musicians are those who manage to incorporate their musical imagination and feeling into their striving for willful technical control. This is wherein lies the magic of great improvisation. Feel it. Hear it.

8. All examples in this book sound great with either a clean or distored tone.

THE FIVE FUNDAMENTAL MINOR PENTATONIC "BOX" SCALE FINGERINGS

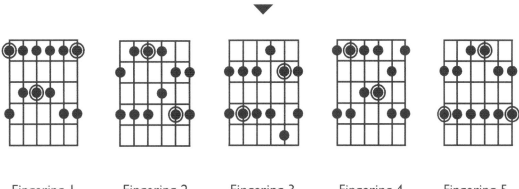

Fingering 1   Fingering 2   Fingering 3   Fingering 4   Fingering 5

section ONE

horizontal shifting

The studies in this section develop multiple pentatonic pathways that move the player's hand **ALONG THE NECK**, which I call **HORIZONTAL MOTION** (since the hand is moving parallel to the earth's horizon, side-to-side.) This is the secret key to unlocking whole neck pentatonic freedom.

There are five fundamental non-shifting pentatonic scale patterns on the guitar. The main characteristic of these patterns is the fact that they have two notes on every string, which creates their "box-like" nature. This section explores different ways to connect these box patterns, **USING A SLIDE** up or down to get from one box pattern into an adjacent box pattern.

In learning these studies, the student will likely encounter certain places where the best choice of fingering will not be obvious. As you work through the exercises, fingerings are suggested, but the student should choose the fingerings that works best for his/her hand. Intelligent choice of fingerings is extremely important, so that execution of the passage is free of 'glitched' notes. Remember, choice of fingering is ultimately up to you. Choose wisely.

Play these melodic studies repetitively and continuously over the accompaniment tracks for a period of weeks and months. We are building an entirely new way of moving across the fretboard, which will take sufficient time and study to assimilate. It is extremely important to become immersed in these exercises on a daily basis, in order to develop absolute whole neck proficiency with this type on pentatonic motion. The exercises in this chapter are a fundamental building block in the development of whole neck freedom. Unlock the magic!

important points for study

▶ Before starting, be sure you know all five pentatonic box scale patterns in two keys: 1) key of E Major/C♯ Minor; and 2) key of A Major/F♯ Minor. All examples in this section are in one of these two keys.

▶ Please begin with Sequence Pattern #1, and learn ALL FIVE studies using this sequence before moving on. This will provide much insight into the layout and scheme of this chapter. Each sequence pattern is demonstrated in five studies because any given sequence can be started from any one of the five pentatonic fingerings. Learning all five studies on a given sequence completes the whole neck system. Ideally, all five studies would be presented in one key in order to demonstrate the coherence of this system. However, two keys were used to keep the hand in the more common playing register.

▶ As you work on these position-shifting exercises, remember to continually practice looking ahead to the upcoming pentatonic box scale pattern before your hand gets there. This is critically important.

▶ The fingerings indicated are those preferred by the author, but ultimately, the student must decide on the fingerings that work best for him. The most recurring problematic fingering decisions are on certain passages where 1) the choice is between using either the 3rd or the 4th finger on an ascending sliding shift; or 2) the choice is between using either the 1st or 2nd finger on a descending sliding shift (the 1st is usually better here).

▶ In practicing all of the initial exercises (Sequence Patterns #1-6), first begin with a 16th note feel. Practice with a metronome, 4 notes-per-click (or 2 notes-per-click initially to work up to 4 eventually). After mastering that, try going to a triplet feel, playing either 3 or 6 notes per click. Set the metronome as slow as you need to in order to practice without mistakes. Muscle memory imprinting at slow speeds gives you the power to control the patterns at faster tempos later. Imprint an exercise at slow speeds for days. It works!

▶ Most exercises can be played with either a 16th note feel or a triplet feel. Occasionally, instructions are indicated to either add or omit notes (at the end of a given line) in order to adapt a 16th note feel to triplets. This is so the overall number of notes in a repeating study will be divisible by three, thus supporting triplets.

▶ Play exercises over backing Tracks No. 6 (in E major/C♯ minor) and No. 7 (in A major/F♯ minor).

> **USE STRICT ALTERNATE PICKING ON ALL EXAMPLES, AS DESCRIBED IN THE APPENDIX OF THIS BOOK!!!**

sequence pattern #1 (5 studies)

This sequence uses a 6-note motif. Play with both a 16th and a triplet feel. Play repetitively over the accompaniment tracks.

 ▶ **No. 1** Study 1 (E Major/C♯ minor)

 ▶ **No. 2** Study 2 (E Major/C♯ minor)

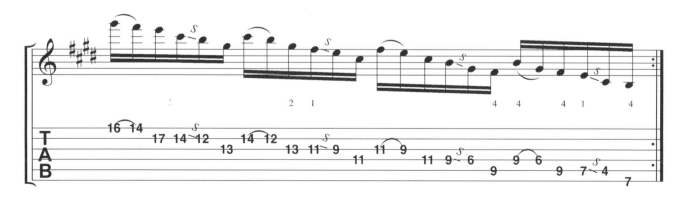

▸ **No. 3** Study 3 (E Major/C♯ minor)

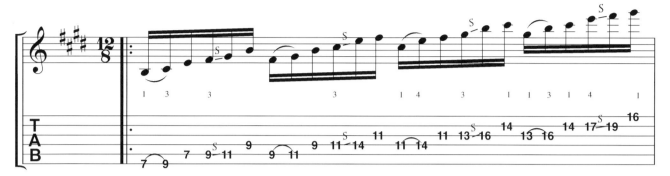

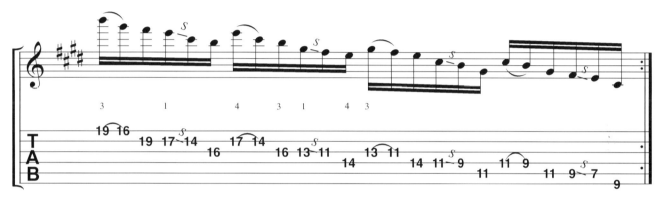

 ▸ **No. 4** Study 4 (A Major/F♯ minor)

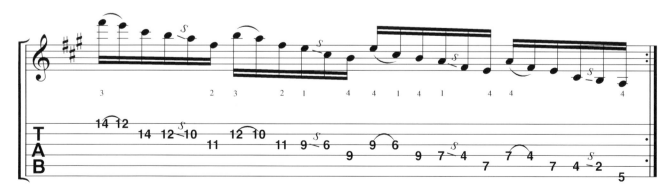

No. 5 Study 5 (A Major/F♯ minor)

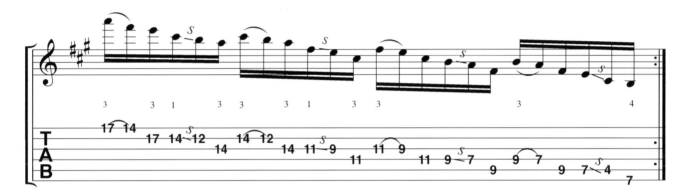

A "sequence" is a mathematical order that is applied to a scale, creating an organized way of progressing through the scale that is more interesting than simply playing it in a straight ascending or descending fashion. For example, if the instructions indicate a "6-note motif" (as in Sequence #1), look for a pattern that repeats every six notes as the exercise progresses.

No. 6 Accompaniment Track in E Major/C♯ minor)

No. 7 Accompaniment Track in A Major/F♯ minor)

sequence pattern #2 (5 studies)

This sequence uses a 8-note motif. Play with both a 16th and a triplet feel. Play over accompaniment tracks. The first note does not get picked on repeats.

 ▸ **No. 8** Study 1 (E Major/C♯ minor)

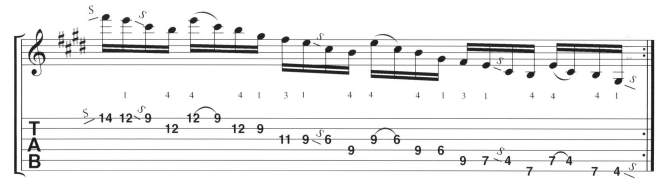

 ▸ **No. 9** Study 2 (E Major/C♯ minor)

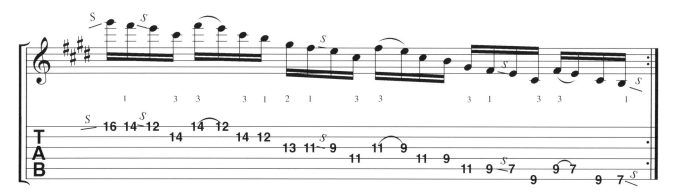

No. 10 Study 3 (E Major/C# minor)

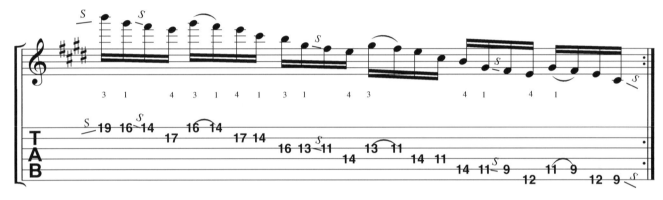

No. 11 Study 4 (A Major/F# minor)

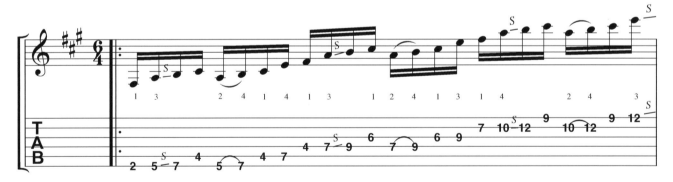

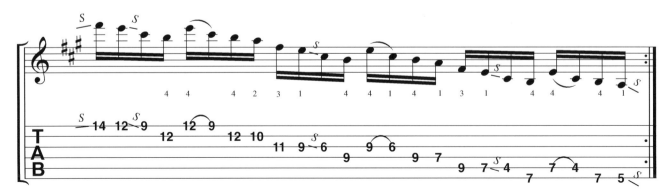

▶ **No. 12** Study 5 (A Major/F♯ minor)

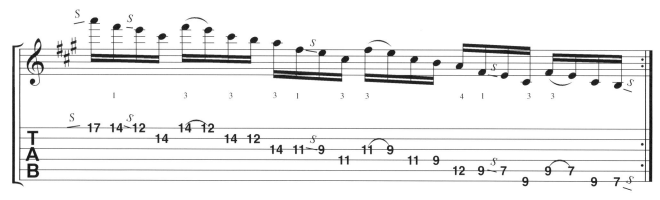

sequence pattern #3 (5 studies)

This sequence uses a 7-note motif. Play in 16ths at first. For triplets, omit the last two notes on each line.

 ▸ **No. 13** Study 1 (E Major/C# minor)

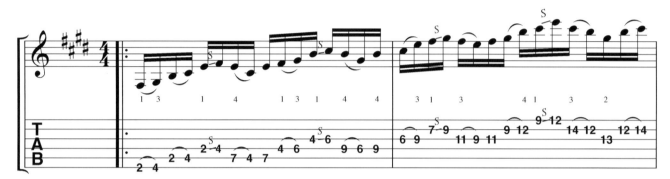

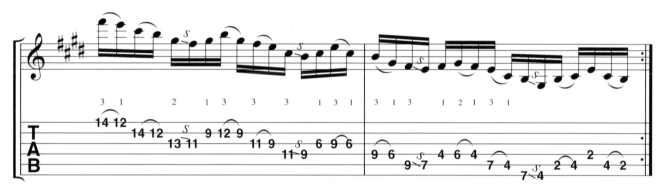

 ▸ **No. 14** Study 2 (E Major/C# minor)

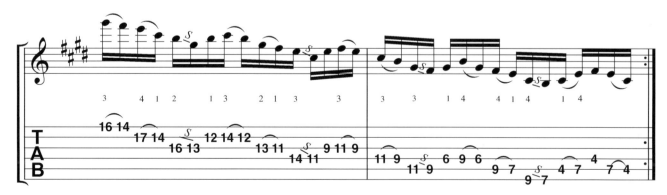

No. 15 Study 3 (E Major/C♯ minor)

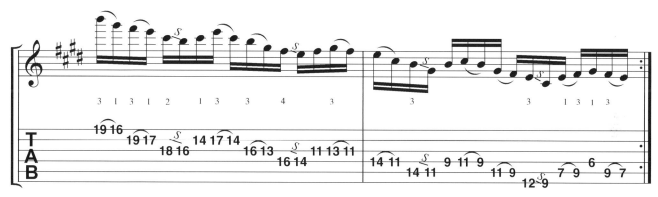

No. 16 Study 4 (A Major/F♯ minor)

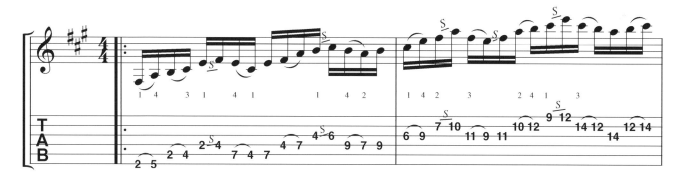

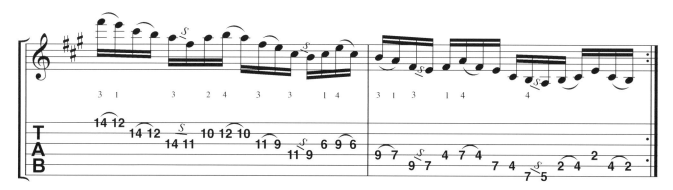

▶ **No. 17** Study 5 (A Major/F♯ minor)

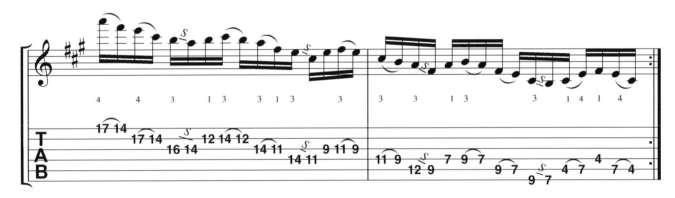

sequence pattern #4 (5 studies)

This sequence uses a 9-note motif. Practice with both a 16th note and a triplet feel.

 ▶ **No. 18** Study 1 (E Major/C# minor)

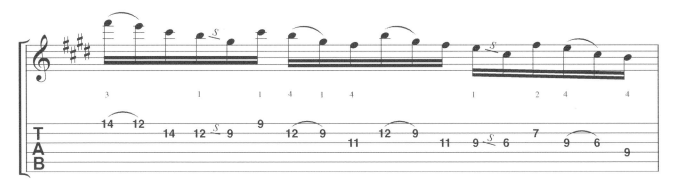

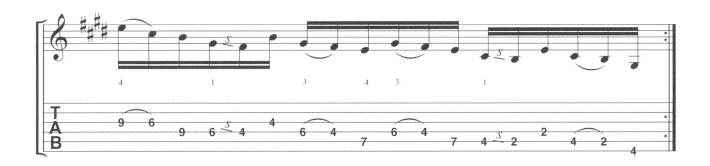

▶ **No. 19** Study 2 (E Major/C# minor)

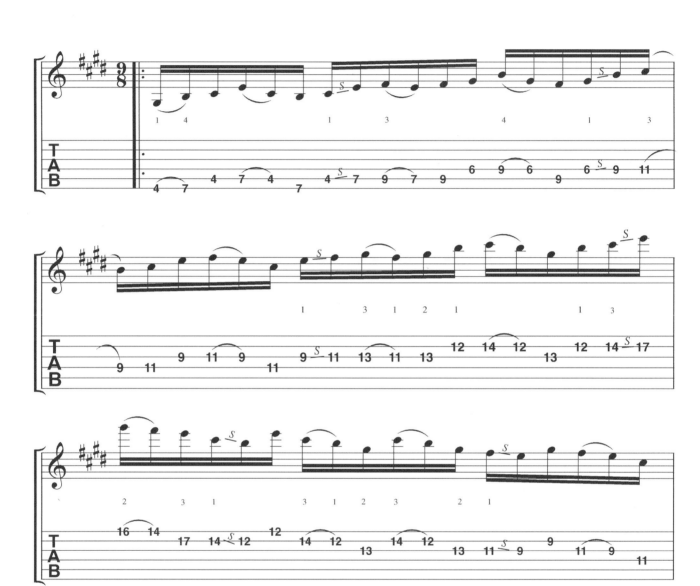

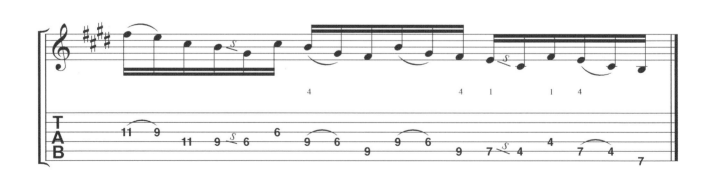

No. 20 Study 3 (E Major/C# minor)

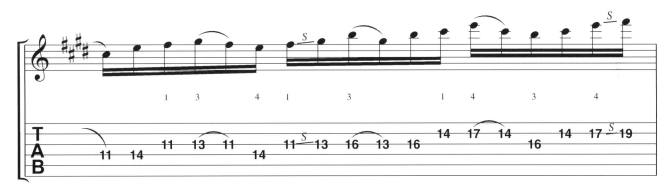

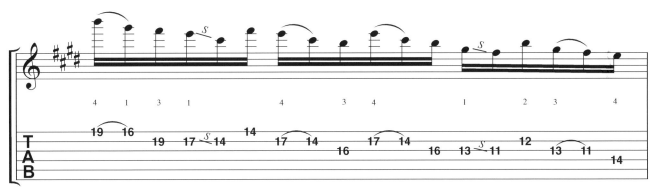

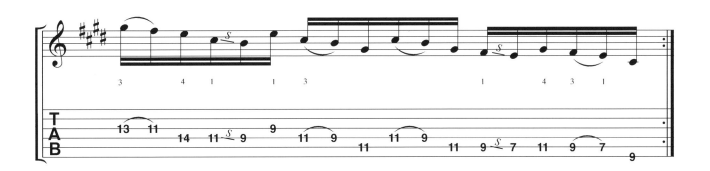

▸ **No. 21** Study 4 (A Major/F♯ minor)

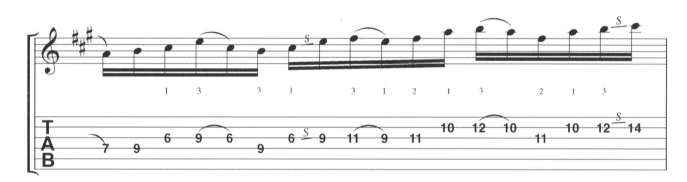

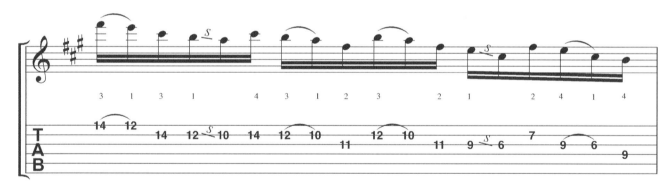

▶ No. 22 Study 5 (A Major/F# minor)

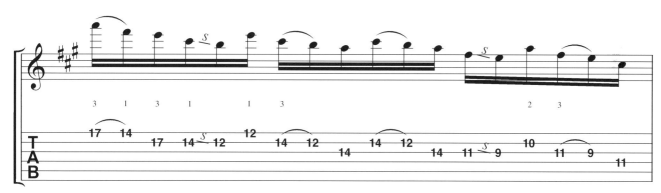

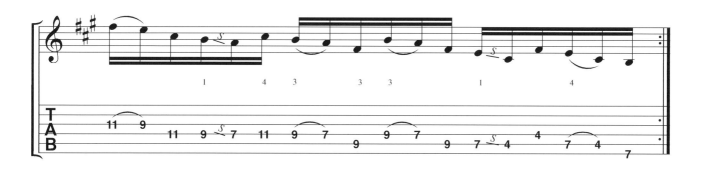

sequence pattern #5 (5 studies)

This sequence uses a 7-note motif. Practice with both a 16th note and a triplet feel.

 ▸ **No. 23** Study 1 (E Major/C♯ minor)

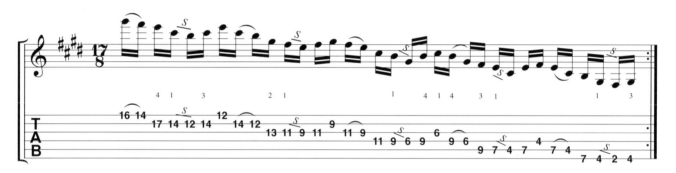

 ▸ **No. 24** Study 2 (E Major/C♯ minor)

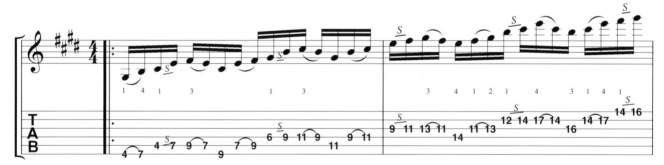

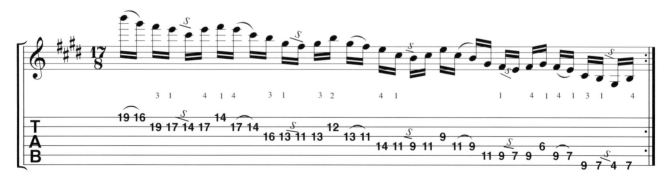

No. 25 Study 3 (E Major/C# minor)

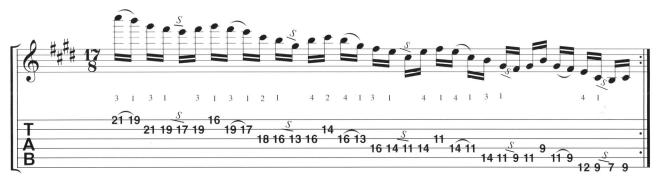

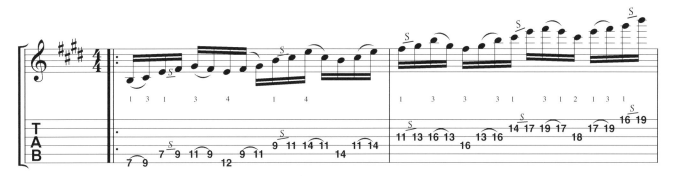

No. 26 Study 4 (A Major/F# minor)

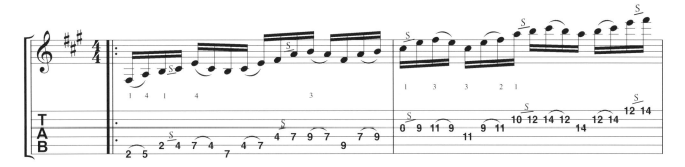

▶ **No. 27** Study 5 (A Major/F♯ minor)

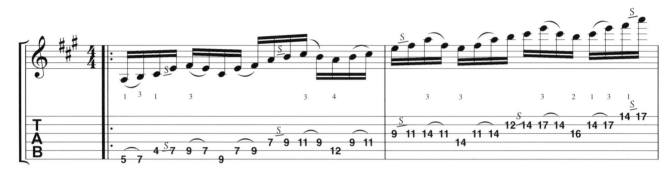

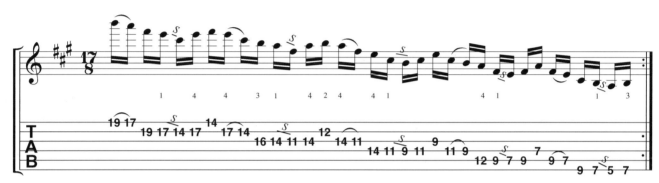

sequence pattern #6 (5 studies)

(7-note ascending motif / 5-note descending motif). Works in both 16th note and a triplet feel.

 No. 28 Study 1 (E Major/C♯ minor)

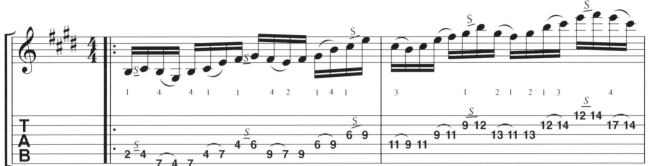

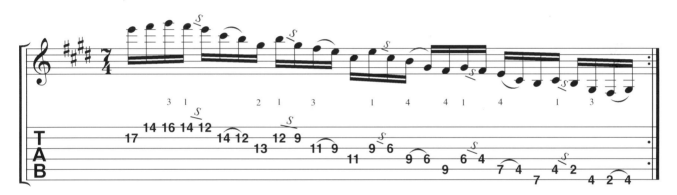

 No. 29 Study 2 (E Major/C♯ minor)

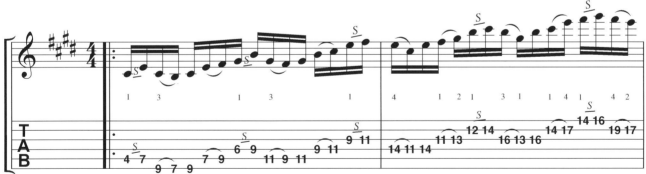

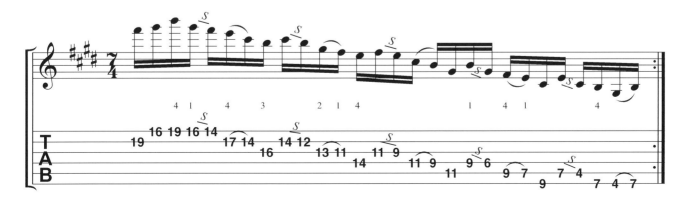

▶ **No. 30** Study 3 (E Major/C♯ minor)

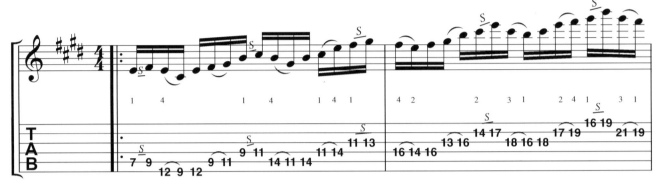

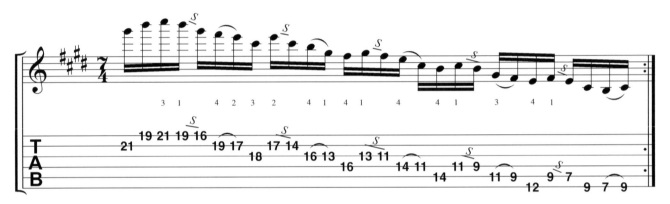

 ▶ **No. 31** Study 4 (A Major/F♯ minor)

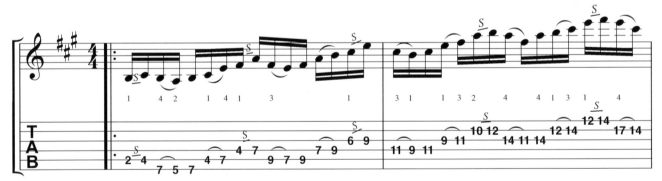

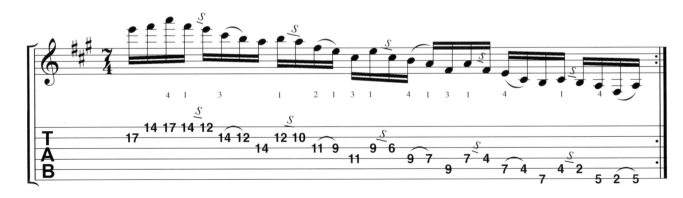

▶ **No. 32** Study 5 (A Major/F♯ minor)

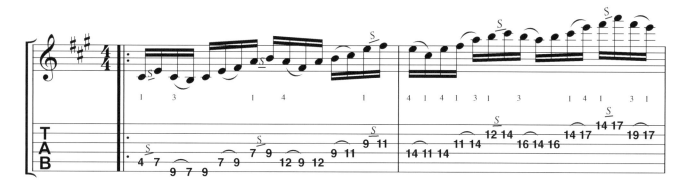

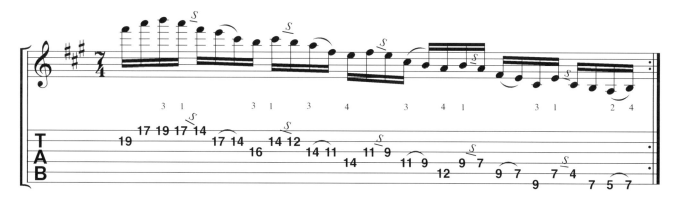

sequence pattern #7 (5 studies)

This study shows reverse horizontal motion. Play with a 16th note feel.

 ▶ **No. 33** Study 1 (E Major/C♯ minor)

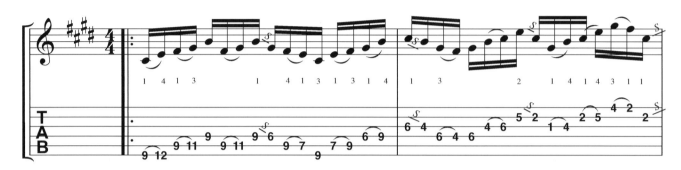

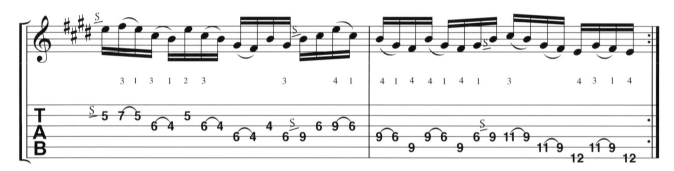

 ▶ **No. 34** Study 2 (E Major/C♯ minor)

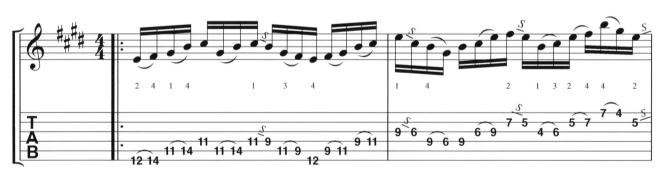

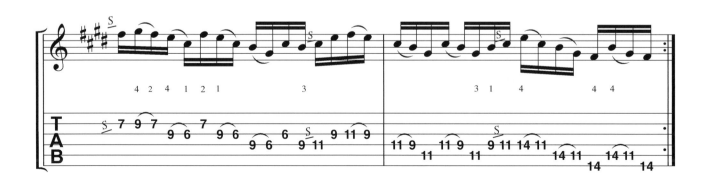

▶ **No. 35** Study 3 (E Major/C♯ minor)

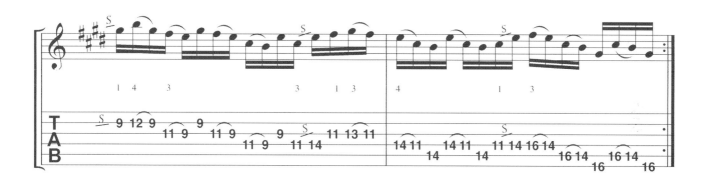

▶ **No. 36** Study 4 (A Major/F♯ minor)

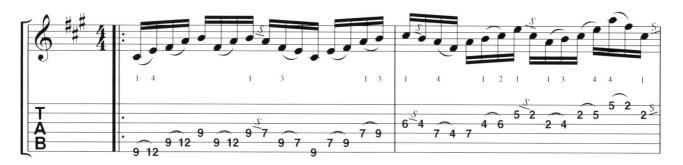

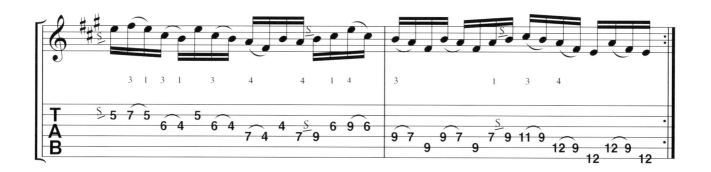

▶ No. 37 Study 5 (A Major/F♯ minor)

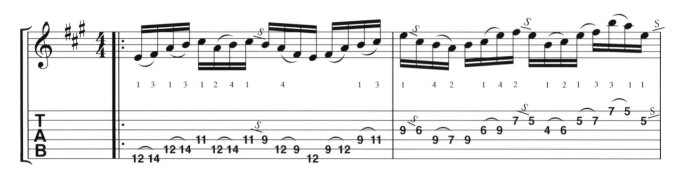

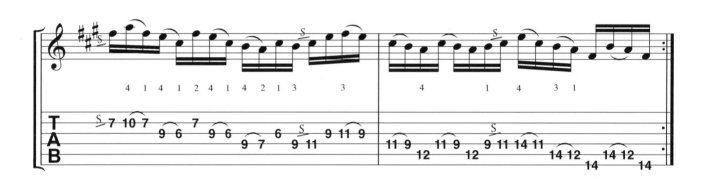

section TWO

non-shifting sequences

important points for study

▶ This section develops another kind of sequential pentatonic motion, where the hand moves **ACROSS THE FRETBOARD** (non-shifting motion where the fretting hand remains *entirely in one position on the neck*). All 15 exercises in this section are repeating, continuous motion studies, and all exercises are presented in the following pentatonic box scale fingering in the key of E Major/C♯ Minor:

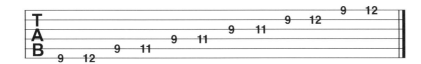

▶ While all exercises are presented in only one of the five pentatonic scale fingerings, the student MUST apply each scale sequence to each of the other four pentatonic patterns! We are creating a fretboard matrix that will be complete only when fluid non-shifting motion is achieved in EACH of the five pentatonic box scale fingerings.

▶ So, with 15 scale sequences, each played in five different scale fingerings for the key of E Major/C♯ Minor, there is a *total of 75 exercises*. Do not feel overwhelmed; simply begin with the first sequence applied to all five fingerings, and play them over the accompaniment in E Major. Then move on to the second sequence. Mastering even 2 of the 15 sequences, in five fingerings, will provide much melodic material.

▶ All exercises can be played with either a 16th note feel or a triplet feel. Occasionally, instructions are given to either add or omit notes (at the end of a given line) in order to adapt a 16th note feel to triplets. This is so the overall number of notes in a repeating study will be divisible by three, thus supporting triplets. Each pattern is demonstrated with a 16th feel on the CD, but it is equally important to master the triplet feel on these exercises to remove limitations in your melodic phrasing.

▶ Practice all exercises over accompaniment Track No. 6 in E Major/C♯ Minor.

DON'T FORGET...in picking any example in this book, the strict alternate picking approach is strongly recommended. Strict alternate picking is completely compatible with the use of hammer-ons, pull-offs, and slides. See the appendix of this book for a thorough discussion of this subject.

AND...when fingering two consecutive notes that lie on adjacent strings in the same fret, use the same finger for both notes. Roll the tip of the finger from one note to the other, instead of lifting the fingertip off the fretboard.

BE SURE TO APPLY THE MATERIAL IN THIS CHAPTER TO ALL FIVE PENTATONIC BOX SCALE FINGERINGS!!!

15 non-shifting pentatonic sequence patterns

Motion studies, all in only one of five pentatonic "boxes". (Key of: E Major/C♯ minor)

*The student MUST apply these exercises to each of the other four box scale fingerings in the same key!

Each sequence is presented with an indication as to its mathematical derivation. For example, a sequence with a 5-note motif can fundamentally be broken down into 5-note sections, which will exhibit the unifying idea that was used to assemble the exercise. Sometimes a few notes that do not fit perfectly into the sequence are added to the end of the ascension or descension, according to the author's wishes.

 ▸ **No. 38** Sequence 1 (6 note motif) / (16ths or triplets)

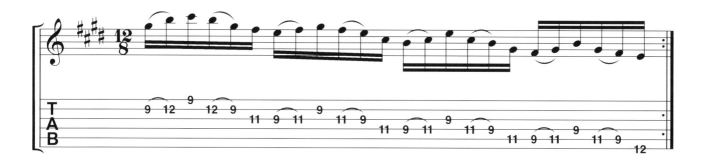

▶ No. 39 Sequence 2 (5 note motif) / (16th feel: for triplets, omit last note)

▶ No. 40 Sequence 3 (4 note motif) / (16th feel: for triplets, omit last note)

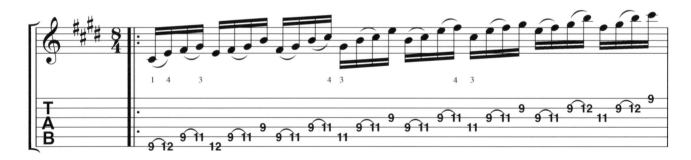

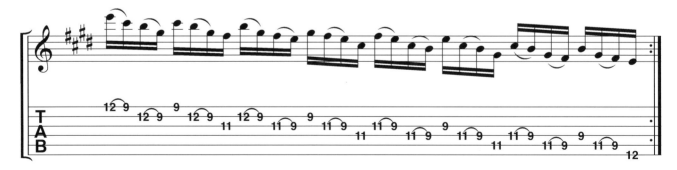

No. 41 Sequence 4 (3 note motif) / (16ths or triplets)

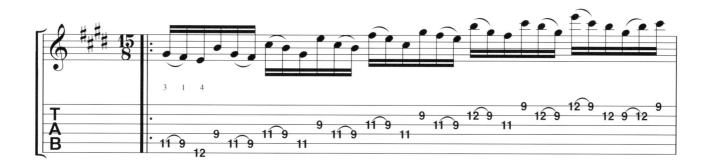

No. 42 Sequence 5 (4 note motif) / (16ths or triplets)

▶ **No. 43** Sequence 6 (6 note motif) / (16ths or triplets)

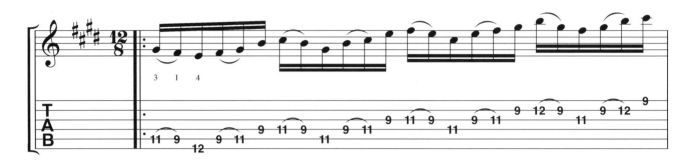

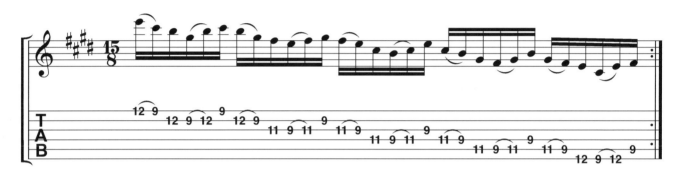

 ▶ **No. 44** Sequence 7 (6 note motif) / (16ths or triplets)

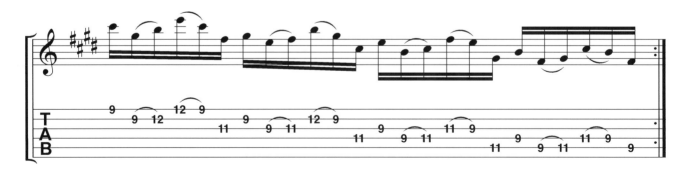

▶ **No. 45** Sequence 8 (5 note motif) / (16th feel: for triplets, omit last 2 notes)

▶ **No. 46** Sequence 9 (6 note motif) / (16ths or triplets)

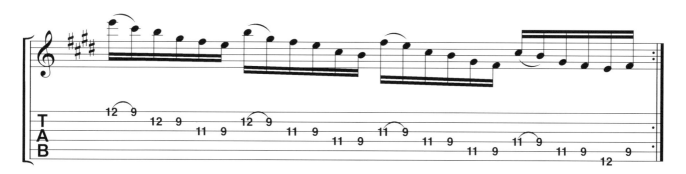

No. 47 Sequence 10 (12 note motif) / (16ths or triplets)

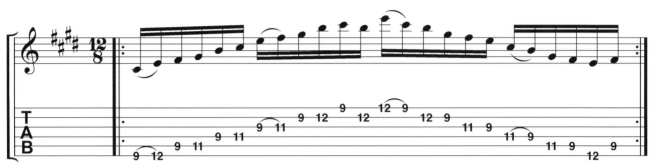

No. 48 Sequence 11 (6 note motif) / (16ths or triplets)

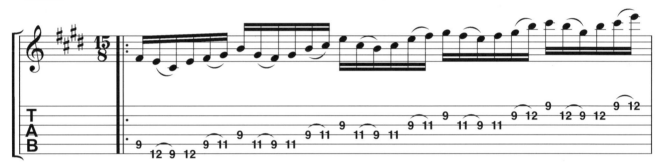

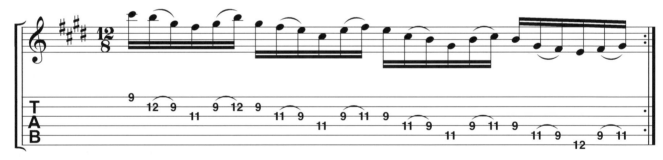

No. 49 Sequence 12 (6 note motif) / (16ths or triplets)

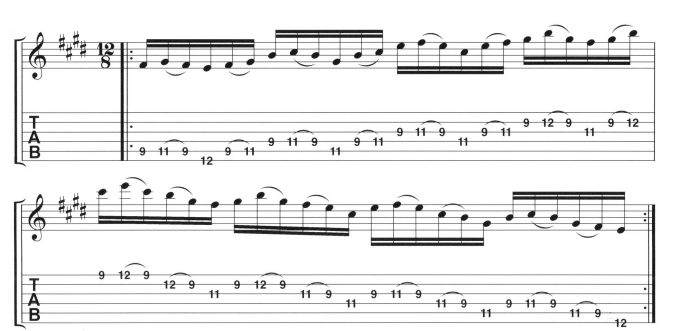

No. 50 Sequence 13 (5 note motif) / (16ths or triplets)

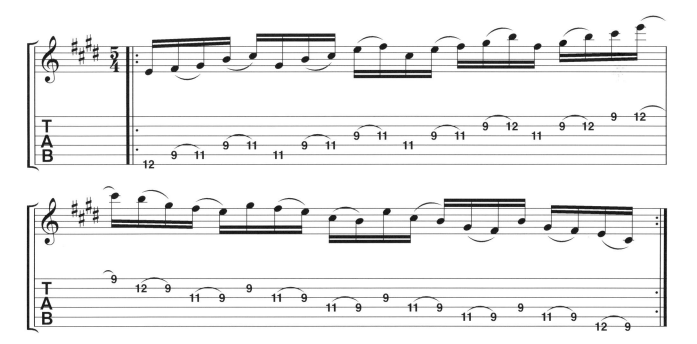

No. 51 Sequence 14 (4 note motif) / (16th feel: for triplets, omit last note)

No. 52 Sequence 15 (3 note motif) / (16ths or triplets)

IMPORTANT NOTE ABOUT NON-SHIFTING PENTATONIC SCALE FINGERINGS...

Each pentatonic "box" scale pattern consists of two notes on each string. These two notes will have either one or two blank frets between them. When the spacing of one fret between the notes occurs on two adjacent strings (creating a parallel box shape), most good pentatonic players will use the 1st and 3rd fingers to fret these notes, even if this results in a slight position shift. When that same note spacing happens on only one string in a pentatonic pattern, generally use the second and fourth fingers to fret the notes. Think through this, because it is fundamentally important.

how to apply a sequence to all five fingerings

This study shows how a given sequence can be applied to the other four scale fingerings.

For this demonstration, we'll use SEQUENCE 2, and learn it in EACH of the five pentatonic "box" scale patterns in the key of E Major/C♯ minor.

 ▶ **No. 53** Fingering 1 (as previously presented on page 34)

 ▶ **No. 54** Fingering 2

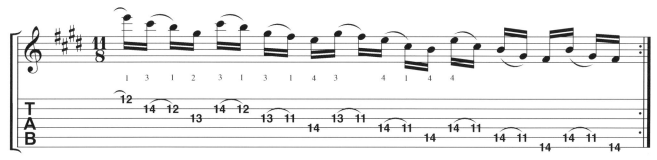

▶ No. 55 Fingering 3

▶ No. 56 Fingering 4

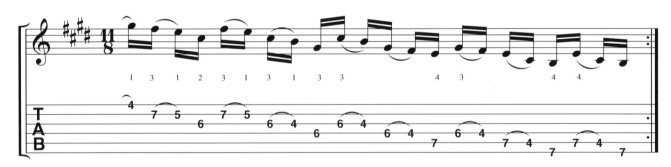

No. 57 Fingering 5

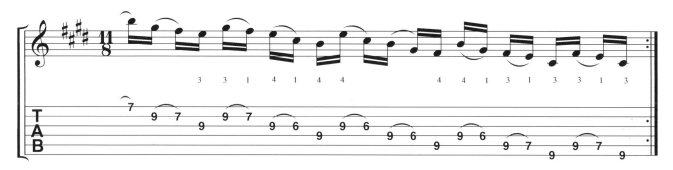

section THREE

whole neck studies

important points for study

▶ These studies combine **HORIZONTAL SHIFTING** with **NON-SHIFTING** motion. These repeating, continual motion exercises represent the kind of flowing pentatonic soloing that is the goal of this book.

▶ WHOLE NECK STUDIES are presented in two groups: (page)

All studies are presented in the key of E Major/C♯ Minor, and should be played repetitively over the accompaniment track in the same key.

side-shifting with pentatonic boxes (5 studies)

Each study focuses on shifting activity between three adjacent box scale fingerings.

Each exercise can be played with either a 16th note or a triplet feel.
All five studies are based on the same template of motion, and and are in the key of E major/C#minor. Play these studies over the accompaniment.

▸ **No. 58** Study 1 (E Major/C# minor)

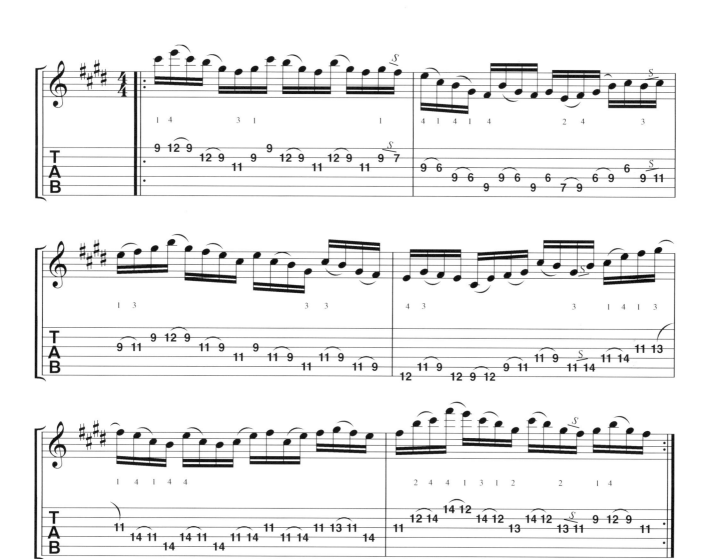

▶ **No. 59** Study 2 (E Major/C♯ minor)

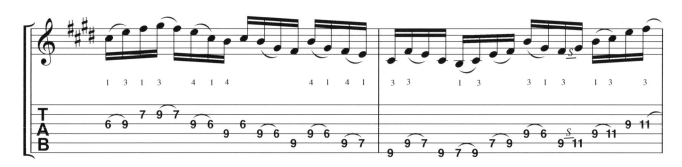

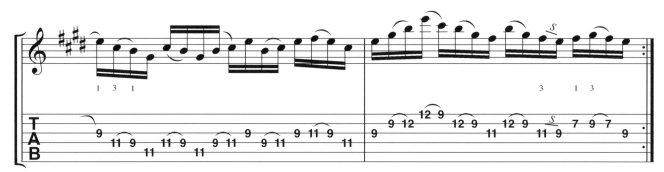

No. 60 Study 3 (E Major/C♯ minor)

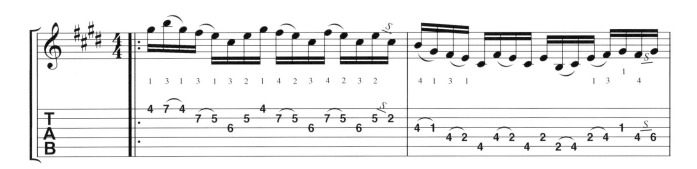

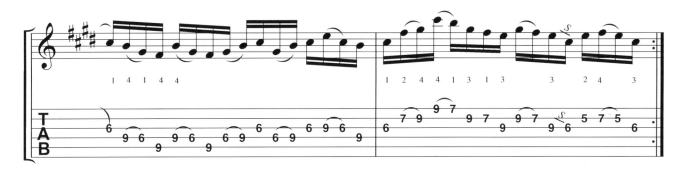

▶ **No. 61** Study 4 (E Major/C♯ minor)

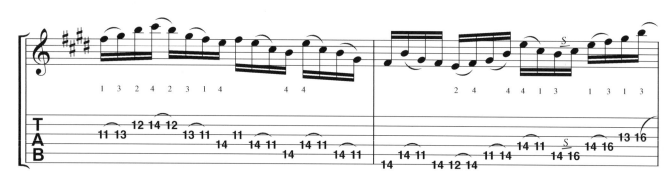

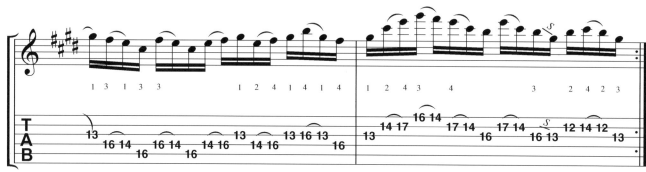

▸ **No. 62** Study 5 (E Major/C# minor)

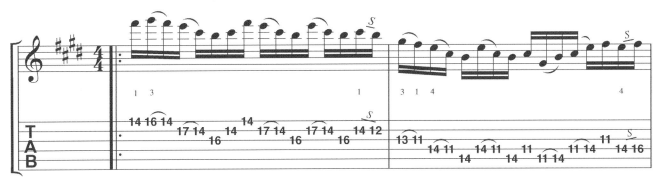

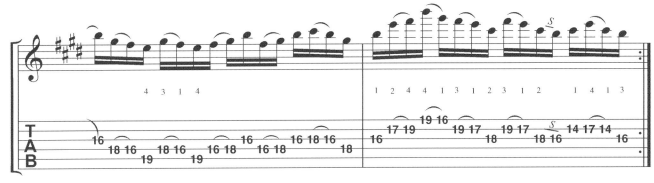

whole-neck pentatonic fluidity (5 studies)

Studies that combine a wide variety fo shifting and non-shifting sequence patterns.

Studies 1-3 are in the key of E major/C♯minor. Studies 4-5 are in the key of A major/F♯minor. All five studies are based on the same template of motion. Play these studies over the accompaniments.

 **No. 63** Study 1 (E Major/C♯ minor)

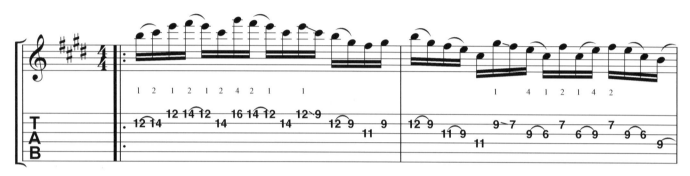

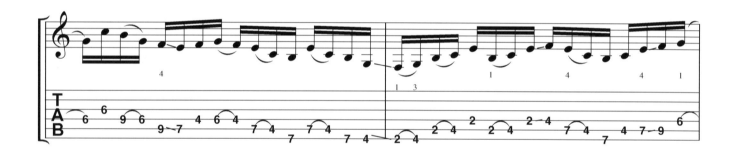

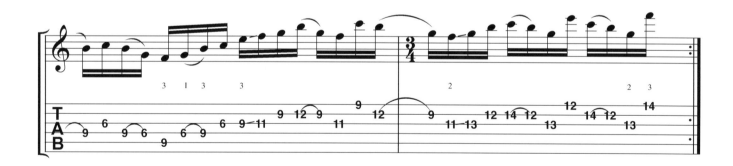

▶ **No. 64** Study 2 (E Major/C♯ minor)

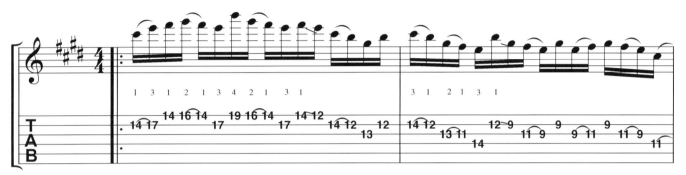

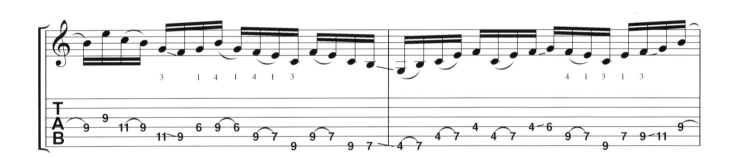

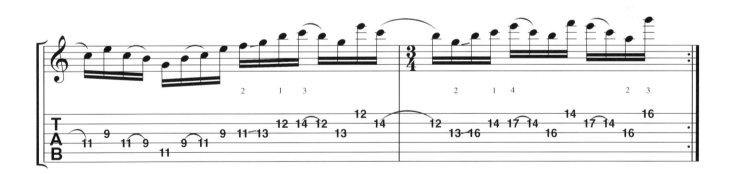

No. 65 Study 3 (E Major/C# minor)

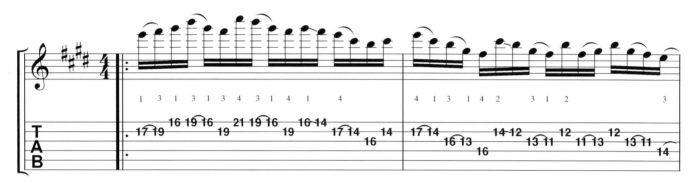

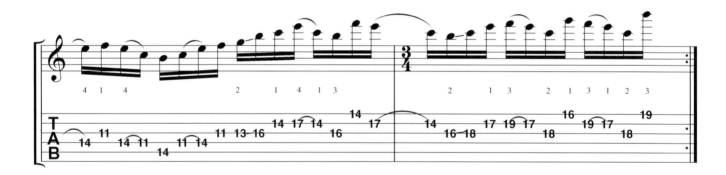

No. 66 Study 4 (A Major/F♯ minor)

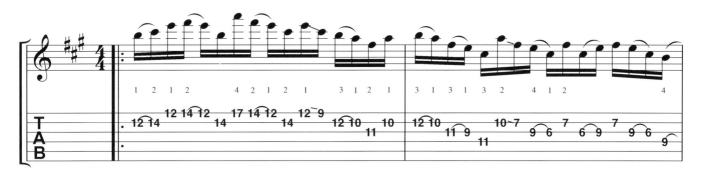

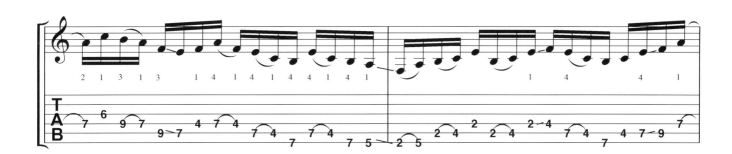

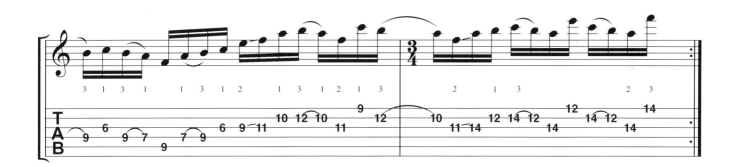

No. 67 Study 5 (A Major/F♯ minor)

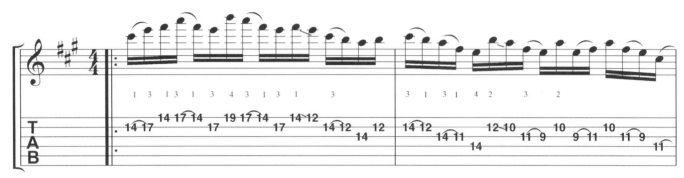

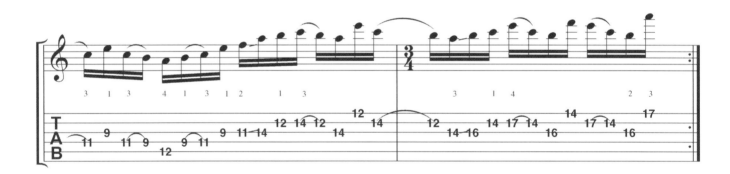

section FOUR

hexatonic studies

The Hexatonic Scale is a minor pentatonic with the 2 added to it, creating a scale comprised of {1, 2, b3, 4, 5, b7}. By emphasizing the half-step interval between 2 and b3 in your melodic lines (using string bending from 2 up to b3), the minor pentatonic sheds much of its traditional blues sound. Rather, the sound presented in these studies is a more modern, perhaps jazzier take on the minor pentatonic scale.

The five melodic studies and the five sequencing exercises are to be memorized and practiced repetitively, as each is designed for continual motion. Hexatonic motion is a powerful tool for improvisation, and yet another interesting and distinct melodic pathway.

Play these studies over the accompaniment track in Eminor/G Major.

▸ **No. 68** Accompaniment Track in E minor/G Major

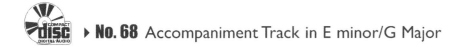

hexatonic scale fingerings

Key of: Eminor/G major

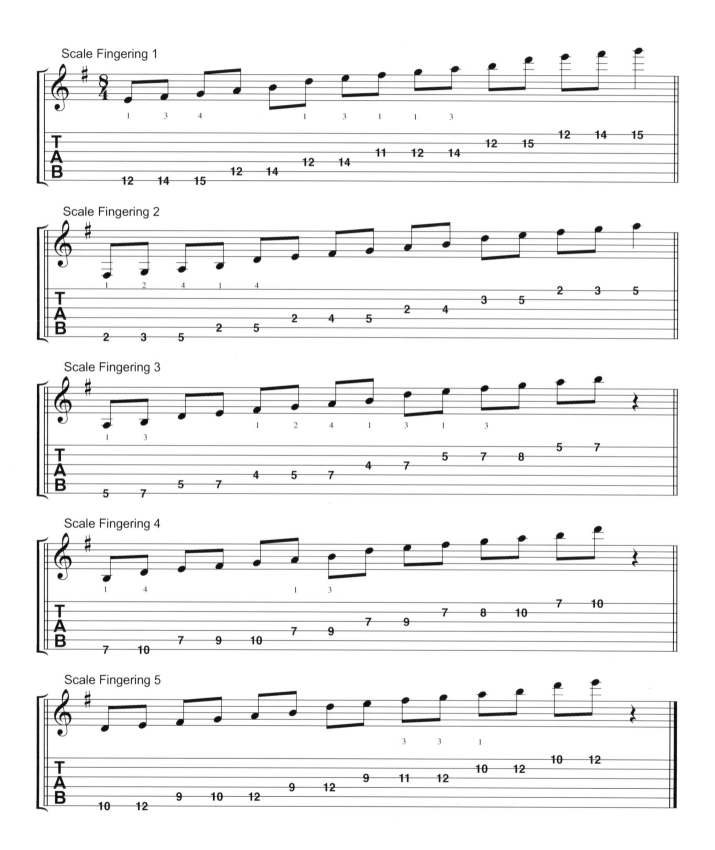

hexatonic melodic etudes

Repeating studies in the key of E minor or G major. Play with a 16th note feel.

▶ **No. 69** Study 1 (in Scale fingering 1)

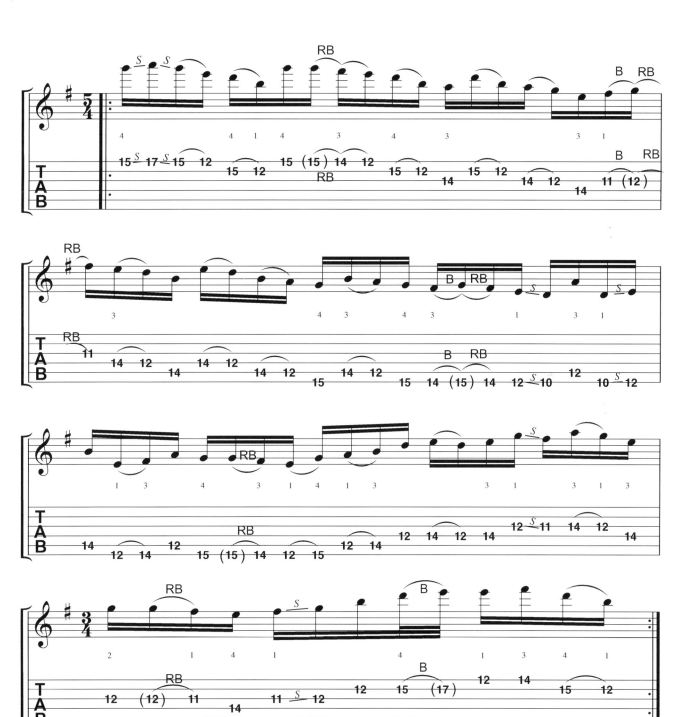

No. 70 Study 2 (in Scale fingering 5)

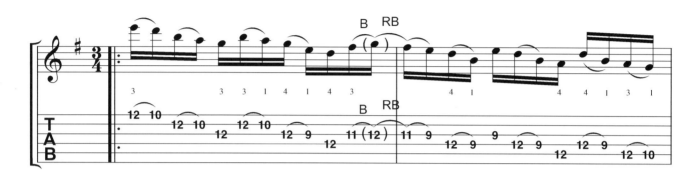

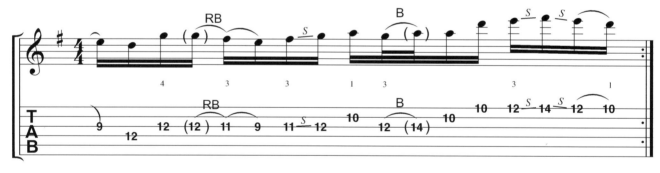

▸ No. 71 Study 3 (in Scale fingering 4)

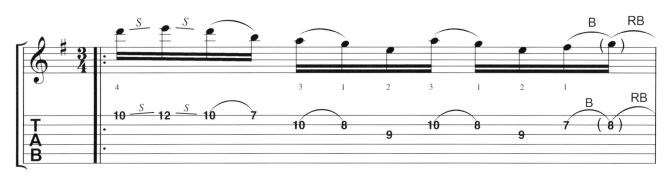

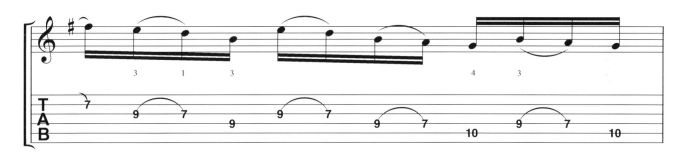

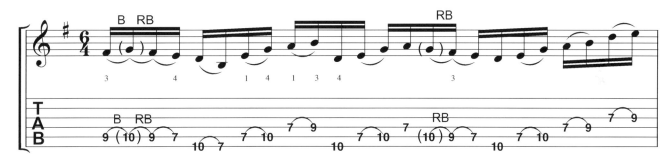

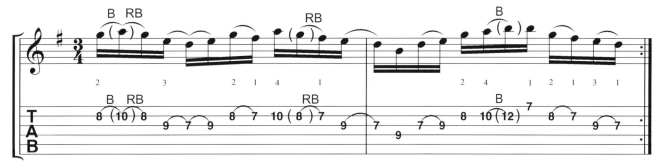

▸ **No. 72** Study 4 (in Scale fingering 3)

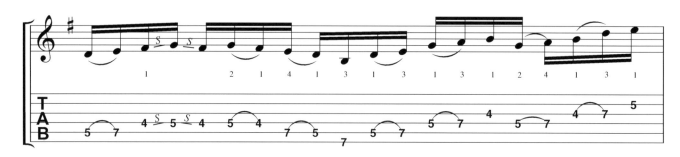

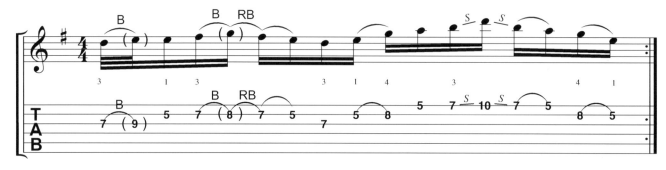

▶ **No. 73** Study 5 (in Scale fingering 2)

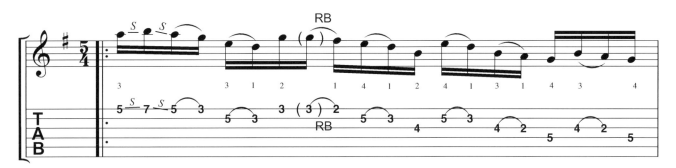

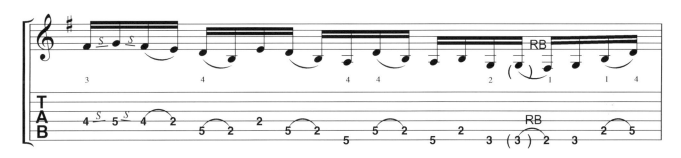

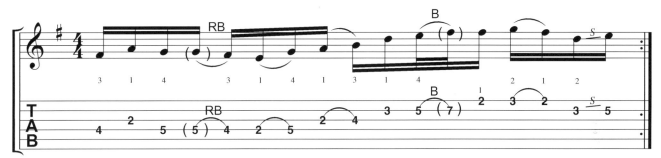

hexatonic melodic sequencing exercises
Angular melodic patterns using hexatonic, but without string bending.

Key of: E minor or G Major.

▶ **No. 74** Study 1 (Scale fingering 1)

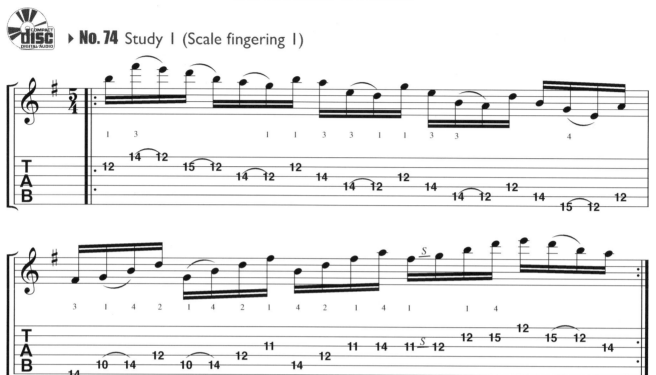

▶ **No. 75** Study 2 (Scale fingering 5)

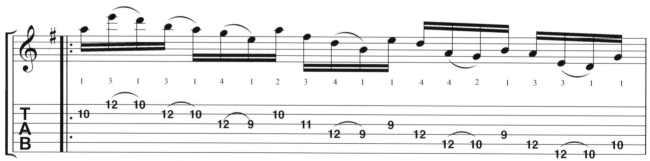

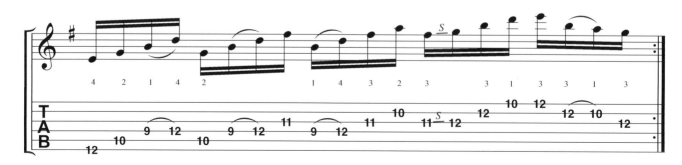

▸ **No. 76** Study 3 (Scale fingering 4)

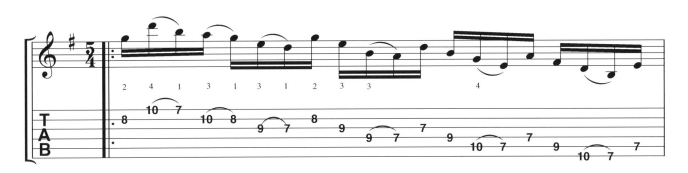

 ▸ **No. 77** Study 4 (Scale fingering 3)

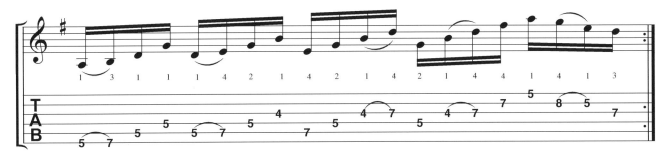

▶ **No. 78** Study 5 (Scale fingering 2)

section FIVE

dominant pentatonic

The dominant pentatonic scale, as I know it, is simply a minor pentatonic with a raised 3rd, therefore comprised of {1, 3, 4, 5, ♭7}. Conversely, it could also be seen as a dominant 7th arpeggio with the 4 added to it. This is a very interesting and useful sound, which could be described as a blending of the mixolydian and the minor pentatonic sounds. Dominant pentatonic implies a dominant 7th chord sound in way that is more bluesy and darker than the mixolydian scale or a dominant 7th arpeggio. The repetitive motion studies presented here feature an emphasis on using string bending between the 3 and the 4 of the scale, a characteristic common among the guitar greats who use this scale, specifically Jeff Beck, Steve Vai, Eric Johnson and John McLaughlin, among others.

When soloing with minor pentatonic scales over a major or dominant 7th chord progression, combine the dominant pentatonic runs alternately with the minor pentatonic scale. The resulting sound is compelling and exotic.

This chapter presents seven different fingerings for the Dominant Pentatonic scale, followed by seven cyclically repeating melodic etudes.

This section includes: (page)

Play these studies over the following accompaniment tracks:

▸ **No. 79** A Mixolydian

‖: A $\frac{G}{A}$ | $\frac{D}{A}$ $\frac{G}{A}$:‖

▸ **No. 80** D Mixolydian

‖: D $\frac{C}{D}$ | $\frac{G}{D}$ $\frac{C}{D}$:‖

dominant pentatonic scale fingerings

Key of: A Mixolydian

Scale Fingering 1

Scale Fingering 2

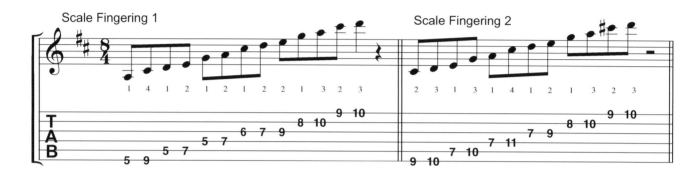

Scale Fingering 3

Scale Fingering 4

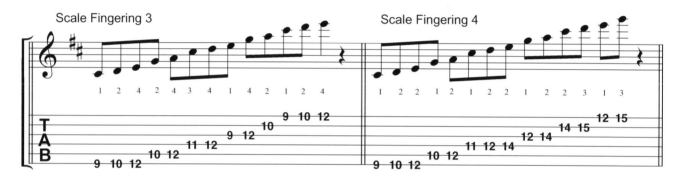

Scale Fingering 5

Scale Fingering 6

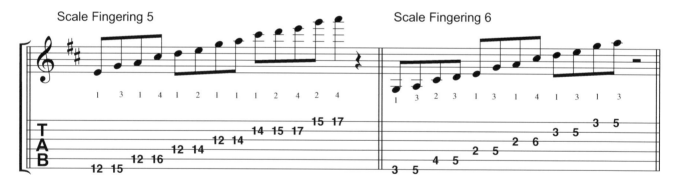

Scale Fingering 7

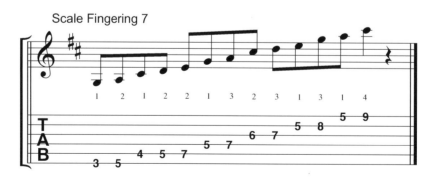

dominant pentatonic melodic etudes

Studies 1-4 are in A dominant pentatonic. Studies 5-7 are in D dominant pentatonic.

Play these etudes repetitively with a 16th note feel.

 ▸ **No. 81** Study 1 (in A Dom. Pentatonic, Fingering 7)

No. 82 Study 2 (in A Dom. Pentatonic, Fingering 1)

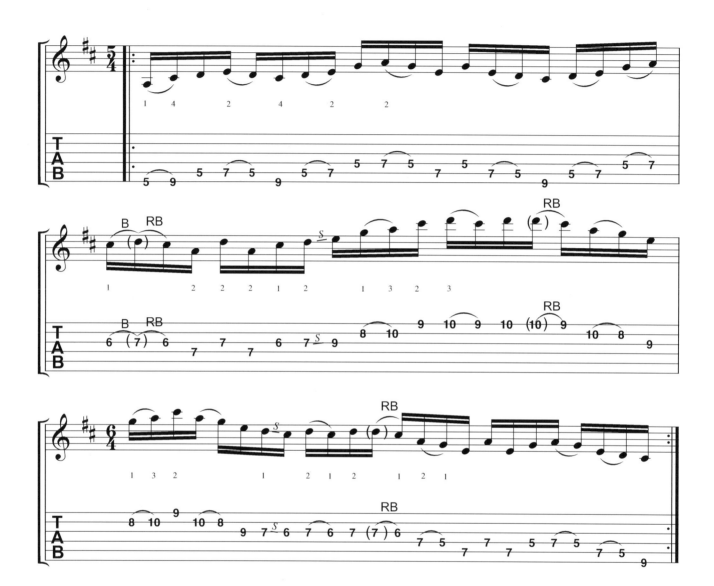

▶ **No. 83** Study 3 (in A Dom. Pentatonic, Fingering 2)

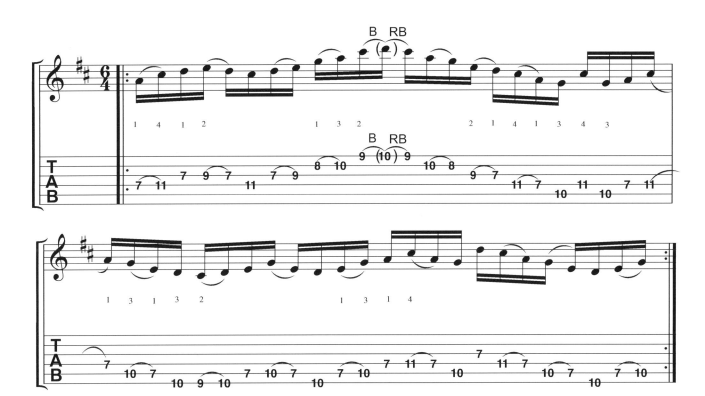

▶ **No. 84** Study 4 (in A Dom. Pentatonic, Fingering 3)

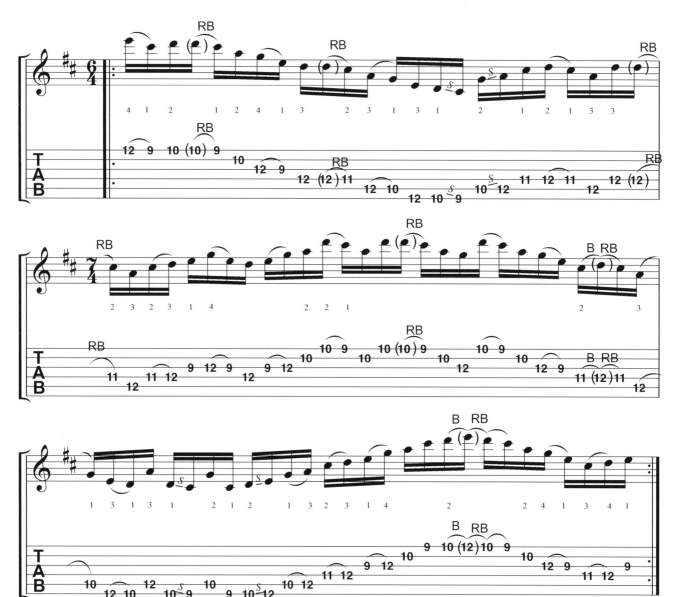

▶ **No. 85** Study 5 (in D Dom. Pentatonic, Fingering 4)

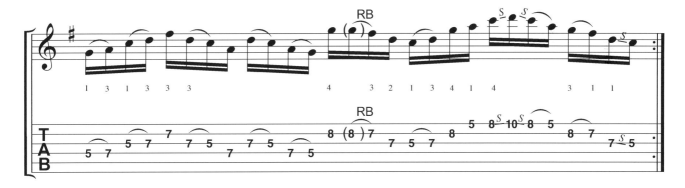

▶ **No. 86** Study 6 (in D Dom. Pentatonic, Fingering 5)

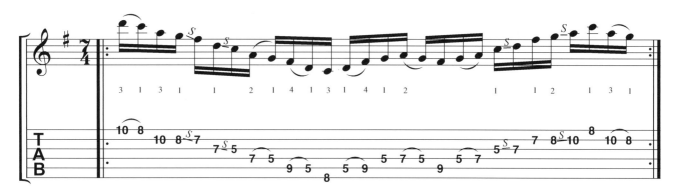

▶ **No. 87** Study 7 (in D Dom. Pentatonic, Fingering 6)

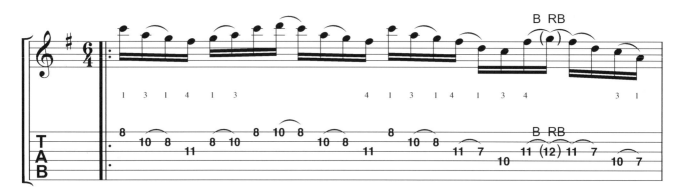

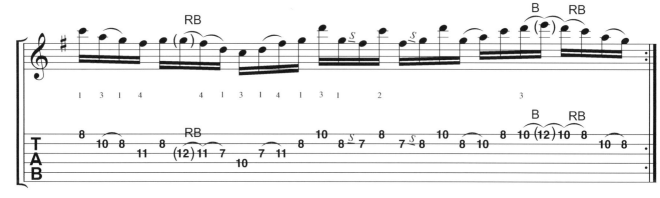

section SIX

soloing etudes

The two etudes presented here are "comprehensive", in that they utilize techniques from this book combined with techniques from the other three books in the "Fluid Soloing Series".

(page)

soloing etude no. 1 (comprehensive)

Combining techniques from this book and other books in the series, to create fluid motion.

▶ **No. 88** ▶ **Etude No. 1**   (Key of: B minor)

▸ No. 88 (cont.)

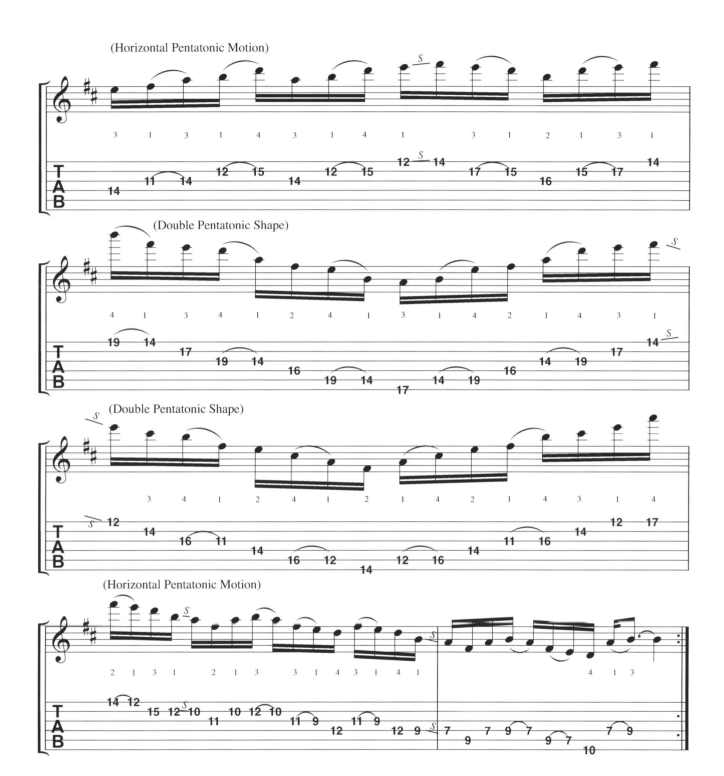

soloing etude no. 2 (comprehensive)

Combining techniques from this book and other books in the series, to create fluid motion.

Chord Progression

‖: Cmi7 | ∕. | Cmi7 | ∕. | Cmi7 | ∕. | Cmi7 | ∕. | B♭ | ∕. |
| Cmi7 | ∕. | B♭ | ∕. | Cmi7 | ∕. | B♭ A♭ | G7 | Cmi7 | ∕. :‖

 No. 89 ▸ **Etude No. 2**

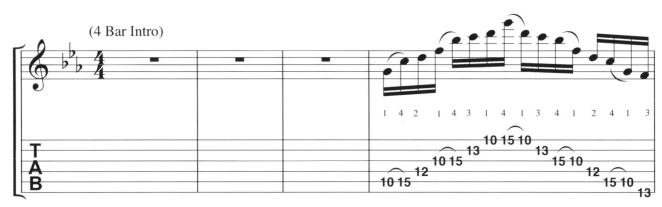

(Double Pentatonic Shape)

(4 Bar Intro)

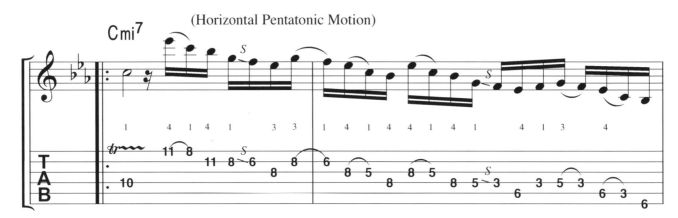

Cmi⁷

(Horizontal Pentatonic Motion)

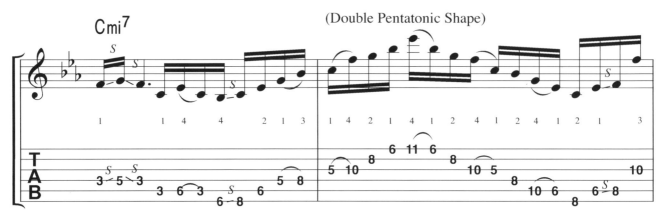

Cmi⁷

(Double Pentatonic Shape)

No. 89 ▸ **Page 2**

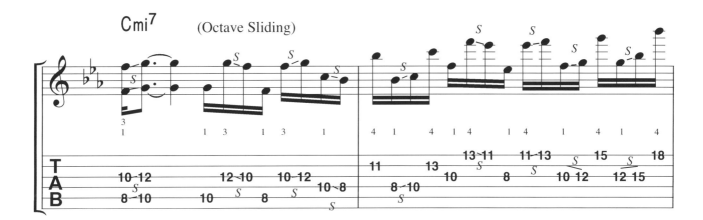

(Double Pentatonic String Skipping)

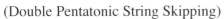

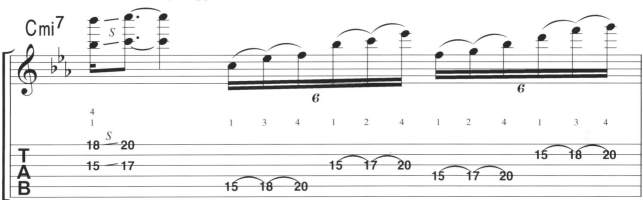

(Extended Arpeggio Run)

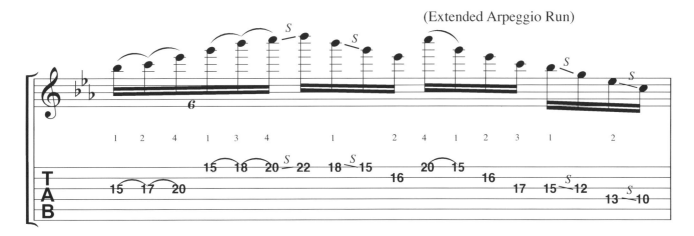

No. 89 ▸ Page 3

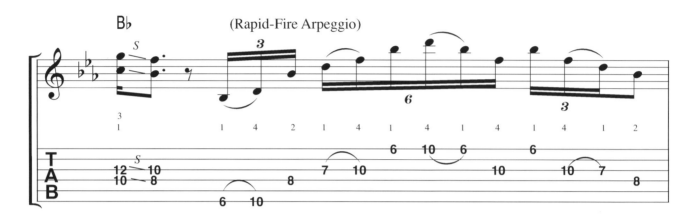

(Rapid-Fire Arpeggio)

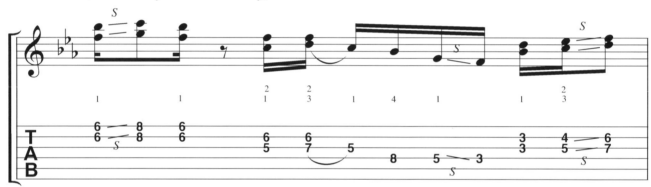

(Hendrix Style Chord-Melody)

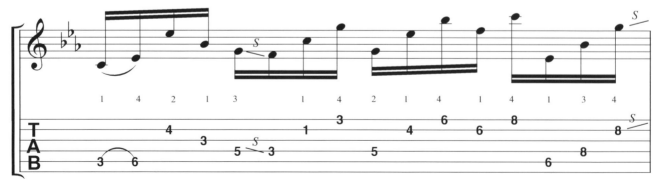

(Rapid-Fire Arpeggio)

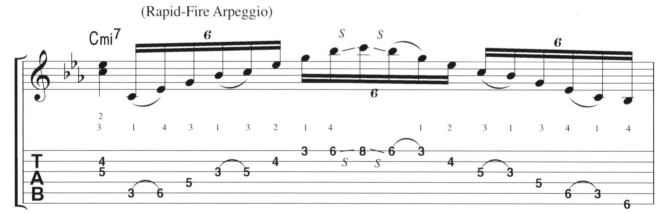

(Wide Interval Arpeggios)

No. 89 ▸ **Page 4**

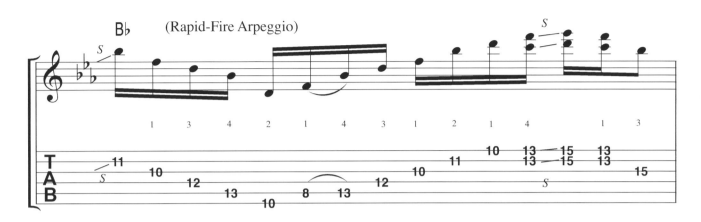

(Rapid-Fire Arpeggio)

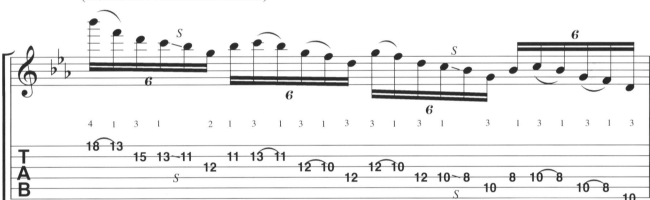

(Horizontal Pentatonic Motion)

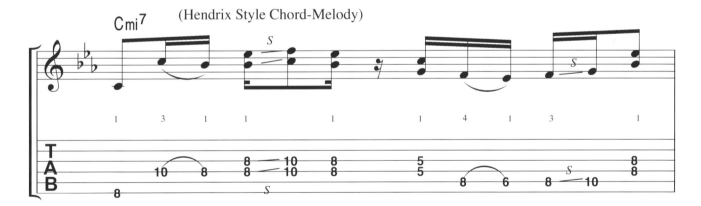

(Hendrix Style Chord-Melody)

(Hendrix Style Chord-Melody)

No. 89 ▸ **Page 5**

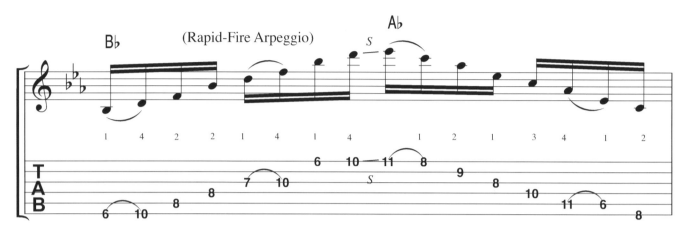

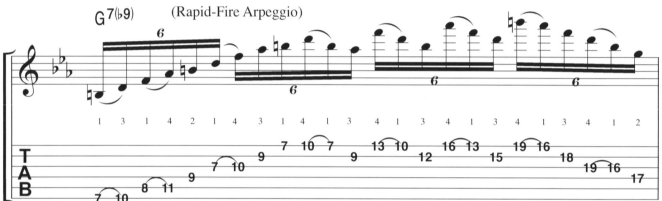

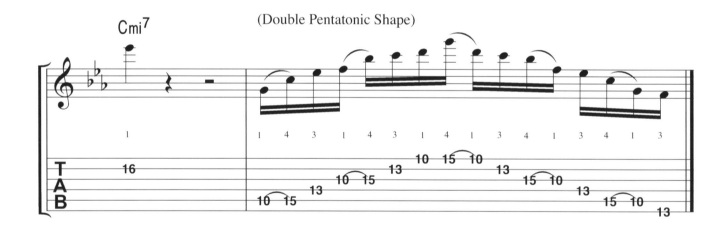

appendix

Guidelines for using this book

Developing Muscle Memory

This book consists of melodic patterns that are designed to increase the guitarist's ability to play fluid, continuous streams of notes when soloing. Virtuosic fretboard control is largely the result of *muscle memory*, when memorized finger patterns are so familiar they can be played almost effortlessly. This gives a guitarist the mental freedom to listen to what he is playing and create music, rather than trying to continually remember where his fingers are supposed to go next.

In developing muscle memory, initial study and memorization should be very deliberate, with careful intellectual attention given to the execution of each and every note in a given study. First, memorize a study. Then, practice it frequently with a metronome at **ultra-slow speeds!** (as in one note-per-click with the metronome on 76 bpm)! While this may seem tedious, it will imprint the intellectual control of the pattern into your mind and hands. This slow-motion imprinting is crucial to developing blazing fluidity and freedom, which will come later. It doesn't happen overnight, but rather over a period of months, as a particular pattern is practiced continually and carefully.

As you practice an exercise at extremely slow tempos, practice looking ahead...to the next group of notes in the study, even as your fingers are occupied with executing the notes of the moment. This is the psychological aspect of musicianship which is often overlooked and underdeveloped...the ability to focus the mental attention either directly on the notes of the moment, or to look ahead to the next group of notes mentally while the fingers rely on muscle memory to execute the notes of the moment. *Consciously develop the mental habit of looking ahead to the upcoming notes.* Each study should be memorized and played repetitively on a daily basis (at both fast and slow tempos) for a period of months, as this will develop muscle memory.

The Rhythm of Continual Motion...16th's & Triplets

Each exercise in this series of books is designed for repetition, so that it starts over again and again without breaking the flow of continual motion. This format is ideal for establishing muscle memory with new and unfamiliar finger patterns. Most examples are constructed in ***either 16th notes or triplets--the two fundamental rhythmic figures for rapid, streaming melodic flow***.

A wide variety of time signatures are used in this series of books: 4/4, 5/4, 6/4, 7/4, 8/4, 6/8, 7/8, 9/8, 12/8, and 15/8. This is nothing to be concerned about, and you really don't even need to pay much attention to it. Grasping control of either a 16th note feel or triplet motion is the primary requisite for being able to apply these exercises to your own music making, no matter what type of groove you are playing over. The unusual time signatures were simply a mathematical necessity, used to accommodate the wide variety of sequential melodic patterns, which may be in formulated in groups of 3, 4, 5, 6, or 7 notes (or sometimes even larger sequential groupings). The goal is simply to be able to play any given exercise in a continuous stream of either 16th notes or triplets.

The Concept of Strict Alternate Picking

In executing slow passages, it is often not necessary to observe any rules in picking. However, when executing fast runs on guitar, it is very helpful to have an organized approach to picking, and among the best guitarists, there *IS* a system which is used more often than not. In its simplest description, strict alternate picking applies to streams of notes in a continuous rhythm, where the first note is struck with a downstroke, the second with an upstroke, etc., maintaining strict alternation. There are two reasons why it is wise to develop alternate picking:

1) **It makes efficient use of picking-hand movements**, which allows for execution of high speed passages; and

2) **It develops a natural inclination to use either a downstroke or an upstroke for each note based on which part of the beat the note falls on**, which results in a consistent approach to picking notes a certain way, depending on how they feel rhythmically, (as opposed to haphazard random picking). For example, continuous eighth notes would be picked down-up-down-up, which puts the downstroke on the first half of the beat, and the upstroke on the second half.

Notice that when you verbally count out loud (either eighth notes, sixteenth notes, or triplets), *placing a slightly harder verbal accent on the first part of every beat helps you feel the rhythm internally*. So it goes with picking. Strict alternate picking uses a downstroke at the beginning of each beat (*except in picking triplets), which makes musical sense, because the downstroke naturally has a slightly heavier attack than the upstroke. Place a slight accent (>) at the beginning of each beat when picking continuous streams of notes.

*(In picking triplets, the first and third beats start with a downstroke, the second and fourth beats start with an upstroke. Learn to place the accent at the start of every triplet, whether using a downstroke or an upstroke.)

Strict Alternate Picking with Hammers, Pulls, & Slides

Finally, we must address what happens to the order of downstrokes and upstrokes when a particular note does not require a pickstroke, as in when a hammer-on, pull-off, or a slide is used. When this is the case (as it often is in the studies presented in this book), the following rule applies: **A SLIDE, HAMMER, PULL-OFF, OR BEND WILL *REPLACE* THE PICKSTROKE WITHIN THE ASSIGNED PICKING ORDER.**

For example, in a group of four sixteenth notes where there is a slide from the second to the third note, the picking order would be down-up-slide-up. The third note is sounded by the fretting hand sliding to it, so the pick would move down above the string without touching it while the fretting hand slides to the note, thus maintaining the organization of the picking order and the rhythmic feel. Another example could be given in picking a series of triplets where there is a hammer from the first to the second note in each triplet. Here, the picking order would be down-hammer-down, up-hammer-up, down-hammer-down, up-hammer-up.

To develop this practical approach to picking, first learn to play a given exercise without any slides, hammers, or pull-offs, so that every note is picked. Remember, it is down-up-down-up for sixteenth notes, or down-up-down/up-down-up for triplets. Also, don't forget to place an accent on the first note of each beat. Get used to the way the picking feels with strict alternation, picking every note. Then go back and eliminate those pick strokes that are actually replaced by the slides, hammers, or pulls (on these notes, the pick makes a "phantom stroke", moving over the string without hitting it). In the initial stages of applying this picking approach to a given passage, *use an exaggerated motion in the picking hand. This makes it easier to simply pass over the string when a slide, hammer-on, or pull-off is used, without interrupting the pendulous motion of the picking hand.* This should initially be studied on small sections at a time, until the picking feels comfortable. This activity is crucial to developing strict alternate picking.

The time spent developing this approach to picking should be considered a worthwhile investment, as it will raise your picking control to a level that allows for maximum speed and fluidity, probably otherwise unattainable. Practice patiently, with determination. In addition, it is also very important to practice reading rhythms with ties, dots, rests, eighth notes, sixteenth notes, and triplets, as you can find in books designed to develop sightreading. When reading rhythms, play them on a single open string, and use the same principal of assigning pickstroke direction based on where a note falls within a particular beat. This activity is crucial to developing strict alternate picking.

Continued practice of proper picking technique as applied to the exercises in this book, and to the activity of reading rhythms in sight-reading books will develop a natural, unthinking inclination toward organized picking. Of course, even after developing this most valuable approach to picking, it is sometimes desirable to break the above rules simply because a particular passage works better when picked differently, although such decisions are best made from the vantage point of strength and control by the accomplished player.

Left-Hand Accuracy and Mental Concentration

Many of the examples in this book require a left hand positioning that facilitates maximum reach and range, such as when a given exercise spans up to seven frets (within one left-hand neck location). This requires that the thumb be positioned low on the neck, and that the left hand be positioned so that it reaches up to the fretboard from below the neck, keeping the fingers parallel to the frets. This is different from the traditional left hand position associated with rock and blues pentatonic soloing, where the left-hand thumb is wrapped around the neck.

In playing a given exercise, pay close attention to notes that tend to be 'glitched'; that is, notes that don't sound fully with a ringing resonance. **You must be mindful and observant to pinpoint those notes that are not sounding fully, and then analyze the cause of the glitch.** This idea cannot be stressed enough. Take the time to observe and analyze the exact cause of the problem, on a given note, within a given exercise. Often the glitched note is caused by not executing the note with adequate velocity on the individual finger that is playing the note.

When working on a given exercise, learn to play it in slow motion, one note at a time. Be mindful not only of playing the notes evenly and continuously, but also of simultaneously keeping your body, hands, and mental attitude RELAXED! Pay close attention to the placement of each note. In this way, playing guitar is very much like the practice of meditation. While you strive to employ your will and intention to control the movements of your fingers, an inner tension naturally arises within your being as you strive to conquer a pattern. When working on new guitar movements, you should periodically remind yourself to relax...to mentally smile from within… to breathe. Avoid having an attitude of striving to impress (yourself and/or others). Playing complex _patterns on the guitar is truly a measure of your ability to concentrate. Concentration translates to your ability to be focused and free from distraction as you play each note_. Distraction arises when you observe what you have just played, and then view it with pleasure or displeasure; or, when you start to think about someone else listening to you perform. This thought process should be released—let go of it. Instead, stay focused on the quality of your execution, on the quality of the sound of the notes.

Look inside a piano, and observe the precision with which each note is sounded. Each hammer, accurately playing each note at the desired moment. Let your fingers be like the hammers inside a piano. Disassociate your striving to play accurately from your emotional review of the results. Even if the notes are not entirely accurate, do not become bogged down in internal feelings of disappointment. And if the notes are performed accurately, do not focus on ideas of self-approval. Always stay focused on the craft, and release internal inclinations of self-approval or disappointment.

As you play an exercise slowly, use the imagery of the mechanical piano hammers. In fact, exaggerate the lifting and independent, abrupt placement of each finger, as if your fingers were like little hammers hitting the strings. _Become aware of the exact cause of any glitched notes, and then solve the problem._ It is a truly simple path, but many guitarists get sidetracked in their mental thought processes before they get around to solving the problem. Have the mentality of being a problem solver. Observe the execution of a difficult passage, playing it slowly with exaggerated left-hand finger placement. Analyze the cause of any glitched notes, and then adjust your hands accordingly. This may seem obvious, but it is actually a level of thinking that is more highly developed among virtuosos, rather than amateurs.

About Left-Hand Fingerings for Pentatonic Motion

This book is presented with suggestions for Left-Hand fingerings for all of the melodic passages contained herein. These fingerings were based on my playing style at the time that I wrote this book, which has been a few years now (between the time of my writing/creating this book and the time of actual publication). This actually works much to your benefit, because I can now pass on to you what I have learned from working with this material for several years after having created it. For the most part, the indicated L.H. fingerings presented in this book are as I originally designed them, while I was creating the material. However, as my playing has evolved with the material in this book (over the past 4 years), I have found myself using less of my Left-Hand 4th finger, with more and more reliance on L.H. fingers 1, 2, and 3. The L.H. 4th finger still gets used (and is sometimes absolutely necessary) but less and less as I get better at this type of playing. You should observe the great pentatonic masters (in ALL styles of music, including contemporary virtuosos, as well as those from the past…from the best classic rockers to the most sophisticated modern shredders), to observe how many of them are able to blaze across the fretboard with pentatonic scales while relying primarily on L.H. fingers 1, 2 and 3. With most of these great players, the L.H. 4th finger still gets used, but to a certain extent, many seem to favor the use of mostly L.H. fingers 1, 2 and 3. ***This is something you should consider carefully!*** Choose your own fingerings based on the following: 1) the fingerings indicated in the book; 2) your own observation of great pentatonic playing by the pentatonic-playing guitar greats; and 3) your own trial and error, and personal decisions. Left-hand fingering choices are very important for this pentatonic style of playing; I cannot emphasize this enough. As a player who plays many different styles, I offer you this valuable insight into this book's modern approach of complete whole-neck pentatonic motion on the guitar.

Final Wisdom

When a given study or exercise can be played with some confidence, further adjust your state of mind, to another level. First, relax yourself, physically and mentally. Then simply listen to the notes as you play them, simultaneously singing them internally. ***Focus your attention on imagining the sound*** of the notes as you play them, rather than on the physical execution. This encourages your hands to be guided by the sound, as opposed to being guided purely by intellectual will. This aspect of musicianship should be intentionally cultivated. Do not underestimate the power of this magical secret.

Finally, be careful not to overstrain the left hand. During intense practice sessions, take timeouts to stretch the arms and hands. If you experience pain from continual and frequent playing, ease up. At that point, you should give your hands a rest for a couple days. To play guitar intensely for a lifetime, one must certainly be sensitive to the periodic pains and micro-injuries that may arise is the hands. These overuse pains (and even swellings) will often disappear if you reduce the intensity and frequency of your guitar playing, and immobilize your wrists and hands (for several days) with wrist braces, available at your local drugstore. Also, playing on a shorter scale length guitar neck (Gibson-style) as opposed to a longer scale length neck (Fender-style) puts a lot less strain on the left hand when working on patterns that require big stretches. That's because the frets are closer together on the short scale length guitar neck. When serious concerns arise with joints and tendons in the hands, do not hesitate in consulting a hand specialist doctor. Take care of your hands, so you can have a lifetime of playing guitar. As a lifetime career guitarist, this author speaks from experience. Now…get busy! (And don't forget to stretch gently.)

All the best,
Tim Quinn

Tablature Symbols Key

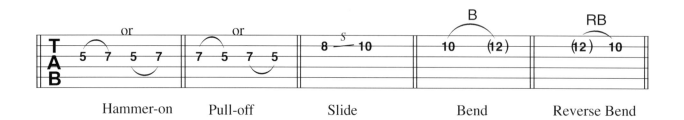

Hammer-on   Pull-off   Slide   Bend   Reverse Bend

MEL BAY PUBLICATIONS, INC. • www.MELBAY.com

WWW.MELBAY.COM